Guest book to celebr

Photos

Messages

_____
_____
_____
_____

Name _____
_____

Messages

_____
_____
_____
_____

Name _____
_____

Photos

Messages

_____

_____

_____

_____

Name _____

_____

Messages

_____

_____

_____

_____

Name _____

_____

Photos

Messages

_____
_____
_____
_____

Name _____
_____

Messages

_____
_____
_____
_____

Name _____
_____

Photos

Messages

_____

_____

_____

_____

Name _____

_____

Messages

_____

_____

_____

_____

Name _____

_____

Photos

Messages

_____

_____

_____

_____

Name _____

_____

Messages

_____

_____

_____

_____

Name _____

_____

Photos

Messages

_____

_____

_____

_____

Name _____

_____

Messages

_____

_____

_____

_____

Name _____

_____

Photos

Messages

_____

_____

_____

_____

_____

Name _____

_____

Messages

_____

_____

_____

_____

Name _____

_____

Photos

Messages

_____

_____

_____

_____

Name _____

_____

Messages

_____

_____

_____

_____

Name _____

_____

Photos

Messages

_____

_____

_____

_____

_____

Name _____

_____

Messages

_____

_____

_____

_____

Name _____

_____

Photos

Messages

_____

_____

_____

_____

Name _____

_____

Messages

_____

_____

_____

_____

Name _____

_____

Photos

Messages

_____

_____

_____

_____

Name _____

_____

Messages

_____

_____

_____

_____

Name _____

_____

Photos

Messages

_____

_____

_____

_____

Name _____

_____

Messages

_____

_____

_____

_____

Name _____

_____

Photos

Messages

_____

_____

_____

_____

Name _____

_____

Messages

_____

_____

_____

_____

Name _____

_____

Photos

Messages

_____

_____

_____

_____

Name _____

_____

Messages

_____

_____

_____

_____

Name _____

_____

Photos

Messages

_____

_____

_____

_____

Name _____

_____

Messages

_____

_____

_____

Name _____

_____

Photos

Messages

_____

_____

_____

_____

Name _____

_____

Messages

_____

_____

_____

_____

Name _____

_____

Photos

Messages

_____
_____
_____
_____

Name _____
_____

Messages

_____
_____
_____
_____

Name _____
_____

Photos

Messages

_____

_____

_____

_____

Name _____

_____

Messages

_____

_____

_____

_____

Name _____

_____

Photos

Messages

_____

_____

_____

_____

_____

Name _____

_____

Messages

_____

_____

_____

_____

Name _____

_____

Photos

Messages

_____

_____

_____

_____

Name _____

_____

Messages

_____

_____

_____

_____

Name _____

_____

Photos

Messages

_____

_____

_____

_____

Name _____

_____

Messages

_____

_____

_____

_____

Name _____

_____

Photos

Messages

_____

_____

_____

_____

Name _____

_____

Messages

_____

_____

_____

_____

Name _____

_____

Photos

Messages

_____

_____

_____

_____

Name _____

_____

Messages

_____

_____

_____

_____

Name _____

_____

Photos

Messages

_____

_____

_____

_____

_____

Name _____

_____

Messages

_____

_____

_____

_____

Name _____

_____

Photos

Messages

_____
_____
_____
_____
_____
Name _____
_____

Messages

_____
_____
_____
_____
Name _____
_____

Photos

Messages

_____

_____

_____

_____

_____

Name _____

_____

Messages

_____

_____

_____

_____

_____

Name _____

_____

Photos

Messages

_____

_____

_____

_____

Name _____

_____

Messages

_____

_____

_____

_____

Name _____

_____

Photos

Messages

_____

_____

_____

_____

_____

Name _____

_____

Messages

_____

_____

_____

_____

Name _____

_____

Photos

Messages

_____

_____

_____

_____

Name _____

_____

Messages

_____

_____

_____

_____

Name _____

_____

Photos

Messages

_____

_____

_____

_____

Name _____

_____

Messages

_____

_____

_____

_____

Name _____

_____

Photos

Messages

_____

_____

_____

_____

Name _____

_____

Messages

_____

_____

_____

_____

Name _____

_____

Photos

Messages

_____
_____
_____
_____
_____

Name _____
_____

Messages

_____
_____
_____
_____

Name _____
_____

Photos

Messages

_____
_____
_____
_____
_____
Name _____
_____

Messages

_____
_____
_____
_____
Name _____
_____

Photos

Messages

_____

_____

_____

_____

Name _____

_____

Messages

_____

_____

_____

_____

Name _____

_____

Photos

Messages

_____

_____

_____

_____

_____

Name_____

_____

Messages

_____

_____

_____

_____

Name_____

_____

Photos

Messages

_____

_____

_____

_____

Name _____

_____

Messages

_____

_____

_____

_____

Name _____

_____

Photos

Messages

_____

_____

_____

_____

Name _____

_____

Messages

_____

_____

_____

_____

Name _____

_____

Photos

Messages

_____
_____
_____
_____

Name _____
_____

Messages

_____
_____
_____
_____

Name _____
_____

Photos

Messages

_____

_____

_____

_____

Name _____

_____

Messages

_____

_____

_____

_____

Name _____

_____

Photos

Messages

_____

_____

_____

_____

Name _____

_____

Messages

_____

_____

_____

_____

Name _____

_____

Photos

Messages

_____

_____

_____

_____

_____

Name _____

_____

Messages

_____

_____

_____

_____

Name _____

_____

Photos

Messages

_____

_____

_____

_____

_____

Name _____

_____

Messages

_____

_____

_____

_____

Name _____

_____

Photas

Messages

_____

_____

_____

_____

Name _____

_____

Messages

_____

_____

_____

_____

Name _____

_____

Photos

Messages

_____

_____

_____

_____

_____

Name _____

_____

Messages

_____

_____

_____

_____

Name _____

_____

Photos

Messages

_____

_____

_____

_____

_____

Name _____

_____

Messages

_____

_____

_____

_____

Name _____

_____

Photos

Messages

_____

_____

_____

_____

_____

Name _____

_____

Messages

_____

_____

_____

_____

Name _____

_____

Photos

Messages

_____

_____

_____

_____

_____

Name

_____

Messages

_____

_____

_____

_____

Name

_____

Photos

Messages

_____

_____

_____

_____

_____

<u>Name</u> _____

_____

Messages

_____

_____

_____

_____

<u>Name</u> _____

_____

Photos

Messages

_____

_____

_____

_____

_____

Name _____

_____

Messages

_____

_____

_____

_____

_____

Name _____

_____

Photos

Messages

_____

_____

_____

_____

Name _____

_____

Messages

_____

_____

_____

_____

Name _____

_____

Gift from	Thank you note sent

Gift from	Thank you note sent

Gift from	Thank you note sent

Gift from	Thank you note sent

Gift from	Thank you note sent

Gift from	Thank you note sent

Guests

_____
_____
_____
_____
_____
_____
_____
_____
_____
_____
_____
_____
_____
_____
_____

Guests

Made in the USA
Monee, IL
26 August 2021